Ten Top Coloring Tips For Coloring Your Mandalas

Coloring floral mandalas can be a relaxing and a creative activity. Here are ten top tips to enhance your coloring experience.

1. Start with a light hand: Begin coloring with a light touch. It's easier to add more color later if needed. A light hand also allows you to blend and layer colors more smoothly.

2. Choose a harmonious color scheme: Select colors that complement each other well. Harmonious color schemes such as analogous or complementary colors can create a visually pleasing result. Consider using colors found in nature for a more realistic touch.

3. Layer colors for depth: Experiment with layering colors to create depth and dimension in your mandala. Start with lighter shades as a base and gradually add darker tones for shading.

4. Blend colors smoothly: Use techniques like blending, shading and feathering to create smooth transitions between colors. You can achieve this with colored pencils, markers or even watercolour pencils.

5. Experiment with different coloring tools: Try various coloring tools such as colored pencils, markers, gel pens, pastels or crayons to see which ones you prefer and give you the desired effect. Different tools can produce unique textures and effects, especially when used in combination.

6. Use white space strategically: Focus on the center: Consider using more vibrant and contrasting colors in the center to draw attention and create a sense of balance.

7. Use white space strategically: Leave some areas uncolored or lightly shaded for contrast and effect and to emphasise certain elements of the design. White space can prevent the mandala from being too busy.

8. Add details mindfully: Pay attention to the smaller details in the floral patterns. Adding fine lines, dots or other textures can enhance the overall design and make your mandala more visually interesting.

9. Consider the background elements: Think about the background of your mandala. You could color it in a solid color, create a gradient, or add a subtle pattern. The background can affect the whole feel of the mandala.

10. Take breaks and enjoy the process: Coloring is a relaxing and enjoyable activity. Take breaks when needed, step back and appreciate your progress, and have fun experimenting with colors and techniques and tools.

Remember, there are no rules in coloring mandalas, so feel free to let your creativity flow and make the process your own.

9 798873 064717